Emotional Growth

A Commonsense Approach to Depression,
Anxiety, and Chronic Stress

FRANK WATKINS

authorHOUSE®

AuthorHouse™
1663 Liberty Drive
Bloomington, IN 47403
www.authorhouse.com
Phone: 1 (800) 839-8640

Published by AuthorHouse 12/03/2019

ISBN: 978-1-7283-3747-0 (sc)
ISBN: 978-1-7283-3745-6 (hc)
ISBN: 978-1-7283-3746-3 (e)

Library of Congress Control Number: 2019919343

Print information available on the last page.

Any people depicted in stock imagery provided by Getty Images are models, and such images are being used for illustrative purposes only. Certain stock imagery © Getty Images.

Cover image by: Deb Baillieul

This book is printed on acid-free paper.

Because of the dynamic nature of the Internet, any web addresses or links contained in this book may have changed since publication and may no longer be valid. The views expressed in this work are solely those of the author and do not necessarily reflect the views of the publisher, and the publisher hereby disclaims any responsibility for them.

Contents

List of Diagrams

A Note to Readers

I have spent untold hours over many years writing this workbook. To the best of my knowledge, the key idea of emotional growth as applied to adults is not found anywhere in the mental health literature, and I do not know of any other work that defines depression, anxiety, or chronic stress in terms of perspective on the past, the future, and the present. Nor am I aware of any research that supports these ideas. Nevertheless, I have put these ideas to work here based on nothing more than my intuitive understanding of the logic and practice of mental health.

I emphasize that this workbook presents a *framework* of emotional growth as described in the several diagrams in the text. My aim is to engage readers in the process of thinking developmentally, which is to say to encourage readers to respond to the exercises. For now, it seems emotional growth is something you do based on broad outlines; perhaps the details will be filled in later.

I have learned from a great many sources though I daresay none of them would endorse this work for which I am solely responsible. (A partial reading list is included as Appendix D.)

Finally, though this workbook presents a developmental model as opposed to a medical model, my intention is for readers to see that the two models are not really in competition. The developmental model seeks to explain how emotional issues develop naturally and thus offers guidance to prevent their growth. The medical model seeks to explain the causes of entrenched mental illness and to describe treatments to reduce their damage. I believe that if we had more discussion about emotional growth, there would be much less demand for mental health services.

Introduction to Emotional Growth

In its simplest form, emotional growth is a practical approach to thinking about and responding to depressive, anxious, and stressful feelings. It is practical in that people with no special training or credentials have access to the principles of emotional growth. They can, in other words, learn the skills they need to grow emotionally. Emotional growth as presented here is theoretical in that its basic tenets can be outlined in terms of diagrams (See list of diagrams). However, the emphasis in this workbook is practical, not theoretical.

Emotional growth recognizes our limitations and affirms our abilities. Its central themes are as follows:

- Troubling feelings are a normal part of human life,
- Our struggles with loss, self-doubt, and lack of focus are consequences of diminished perspective on the past, the future and the present respectively,
- With guidance and support, most people can restore their perspective, and
- When we practice self-care habits and anticipate obstacles we can overcome, or at least manage, most of the setbacks we encounter.

The primary focus of emotional growth is to prevent troubling feelings from complicating our everyday lives. As such, it offers guidance, not treatment. Treatment is reserved for people with entrenched dysfunctional habits or those under the care of medical professionals. Guidance, on the other hand, is for people who struggle with an assortment of unwanted feelings, people sometimes referred to as "the walking wounded."

It is probably clear to readers who have looked into self-help books that this workbook is different. There is no mention of the DSM-V (the fifth edition of the *Diagnostic and Statistical Manual*, commonly referred to as the bible of mental health disorders). Formal diagnoses, the causes of our depressive, anxious, or stressful feelings and the use of various medications have no part in this workbook. Emotional growth is a journey down a very different path as indicated by the following statements:

- Troubling feelings are troubling for a very good reason; they alert you to you struggles you have processing difficult experiences.
- We struggle with issues such as letting go, self-doubt, and lack of focus, but these are long-term struggles not to be confused with feelings. The difference is significant: we have techniques for coping with feelings, but we need purposes and strategies to manage our issues.
- Emotional growth requires two separate tasks: restoring perspective and sustaining the progress you make when

you restore perspective. Restoring is a learning task, but sustaining is an integrating task.

- Unlike the standard view of mental health orthodoxy, you are empowered by taking responsibility for your troubling feelings; it is better to own your feelings than to be owned by them.

Given that this approach is a departure from mental health orthodoxy, what is the basis for claiming that it is a commonsense approach as stated in the subtitle? Advocates of the medical model certainly do not see any of the tenets of this workbook as common sense. Their chief objection is that it blames the victim by suggesting that the mentally ill are somehow responsible for their misery when they clearly have an illness over which they have no control. This argument is discussed later in the text, but for now, it is enough to say that it rests on dubious science and deep confusion about the meaning of the word *responsibility*.

The claim to common sense is hypothetical. It is based on accessibility, not popularity. If more people understood that their troubling feelings were interpretations of the unavoidable struggles of modern life and if the mental health community assured those people that taking ownership of their troubling feelings was the surest way to prevent mental health difficulties, more people would discover the basic principles of emotional growth. They would take responsibility for their troubling feelings, understand that they participated in their loss of perspective, seek guidance rather than treatment, and take purposeful steps to restore their perspective.

None of this requires academic credentials; in fact, academic credentials seem to get in the way of understanding how troubling feelings are part of every human life. The commonsense view is that we benefit from being depressed, anxious, or stressed from time to time so that we can develop new strategies for living more-fulfilling lives.

Why is this important? When we take responsibility for our feelings and our behavior, we eliminate the need to blame, control, manipulate, and be hostile toward others. Who knows how much time and energy is wasted on those activities? So the consequences of this commonsense approach have social implications. When we own our troubling feelings, we are better able to manage our responses to them and to others. My concern here is that the medical model has eroded our sense of responsibility and consequently our capacity to deal with conflict.

Having duly warned readers, I hope they find this outline of emotional growth stimulating and the exercises instructive.

Introduction to the Exercises

The exercises in this workbook are designed for individual readers but can easily be adapted to a group format. They are subjective in that there are no right answers and nontechnical in that no mental health jargon is used. Some exercises introduce discussion topics; others call for personal statements that illustrate a concept discussed in the current chapter.

Readers are encouraged to respond to the exercises in writing or verbally if a group is involved or perhaps both. If you write your responses, you will want to protect them so that only people you trust will see them. In any event, it is important to remember that these exercises do not require you to make moral judgments. Their only purpose is to help you learn to think in terms of emotional growth, that is, to think developmentally.

Chapter 1

A Framework for Emotional Growth

Introduction

From the outset, emotional growth sets a different tone. It rejects the view that depressive, anxious, and stressful feelings are symptoms of biological defects. They are opportunities to explore and learn. You learn from troubling feelings when you

1. Attend to the messages they convey,
2. Identify your issues as a loss of perspective and emotional growth as the process of restoring perspective, and
3. Integrate perspective building skills into your everyday obstacles.

Emotional growth is a process that applies to three separate tasks, each of which is a different way to grow. The diagram below outlines the key elements.

Tasks / Process	Getting Grounded	Restoring Perspective	Sustaining Progress and Accepting Benefits
Problem	You have minimal awareness of your feelings and a diminished capacity for empathy.	You have lost perspective on your past, your future, or your present and hence feel dominated, threatened, or overwhelmed.	You have grown but have not embraced your progress in your everyday life.
Issues	You need to attend to messages conveyed by your feelings.	You need to let go of your losses, be more assertive, and focus on the present moment.	You need to anticipate resistance and accept new feelings.
Skills	You need to learn how to explore and express troubling feelings.	You need to restore perspective on your losses, your challenges, and the turmoil in your life.	You need to prepare contingency plans and practice self-care.
Goals	Have greater awareness of self.	Be liberated from past burdens, realistic about future threats, and focused on the present.	Appreciate the quality of everyday life more fully.

Framework for Emotional Growth

The Framework for Emotional Growth diagram is a map of the different ways you might encounter some aspect of emotional growth. That is, your approach to emotional growth might be *task oriented*; your task might be to get grounded, to find relief from unwanted feelings or to invest in the process of integrating perspective-building skills to achieve personal goals. Or it might be *process oriented*. You might be in search of understanding your core issues so that you can conceptualize them, formulate action plans to address them and discover the consequences of your emotional growth.

As a preliminary exercise, consider which of the three columns you identify with. Then consider how you process your experiences. This exercise will orient you to the issues to be discussed in the rest of this workbook.

Getting Grounded

The Problem

Some people are unaware that feelings exist, especially troubling feelings. For the most part, these people function reasonably well at least in the minds of outsiders. They are spouses, parents, employees, and friends to mention a few roles they may occupy. However, they tend to be disengaged. Not recognizing any emotional problems of their own, they don't relate to problems others might have, so their relationships are tenuous. A deeper problem is that they do of course have problems but lack the ability to articulate them. They become emotional loners feeling misunderstood and isolated. We are regrettably familiar with some of these people from what we see and hear in the news.

The Issue

The problem of not being grounded or being tenuously grounded has a simple remedy: to attend to your feelings or more specifically to note that depressive moods draw you into the past, anxious moods push the future further away, and chronic stress disrupts your comfort zone. Actually, attending is not so simple. It awakens you to the unexpected idea that troubling feelings have a purpose other than to make your life miserable.

Skills

The task of getting grounded is to become comfortable with your uncomfortable feelings—that means being able to explore their origins and patterns in your personal history and to be able to describe them but also to express them in nonliteral language. The net effect of applying these skills is the sense that you own your feelings. Whatever you feel, you are sure that you came by those feelings honestly.

Goals

The goal of getting grounded is not only to have satisfying feelings but also to be able to understand and appreciate your feelings whatever they might be. It is not a goal that is ever fully achieved just as the Socratic goal "Know thyself" is never final.

Restoring Perspective

The Problem

A great many people suffer from depressive, anxious, and stressful feelings.

Depressed people feel dominated by their losses. Anxious people feel threatened by or unequal to the tasks of daily life. Chronically stressed people feel the pace of change in their lives is overwhelming. The problem for each group is a loss of perspective on the past, the future, and the present.

The Issue

Losing perspective is a subtle but powerful process. It is difficult to describe all the developmental features of the process, but its presence in an individual's life is often quite clear. People who have lost perspective on the past say they can't let go of their loss; their issue is to achieve emotional distance. People who have lost perspective on the future tend to say (or act as if) they are trapped by events; their issue is to be more assertive. People who have lost perspective on the present often complain that they can't stay focused; their issue is to stay in the present moment where the pace of change is not a factor.

Skills

Skills designed to let go, to encourage assertiveness, and to stay in the present moment, that is, to restore perspective, are generally well known. Many readers will be familiar with those described here though they might not be as familiar with the role these skills have in restoring perspective.

Goals

Some people want to be liberated from the burdens of their past. Some want to be more confident as they confront new challenges. Some seek peace of mind as a respite from the confusion of their daily life. Restoring perspective by adopting specific skills brings relief from troubling feelings.

Accepting Benefits

The Problem

Some people who get grounded and restore perspective discover that emotional growth is more demanding than they had thought. For some, the surprise is that everyday life is filled with obstacles to their plans. For others, it is their own resistance to change that gives them second thoughts. Still others encounter hope, confidence, and peace of mind and wonder if they deserve to feel better. It is difficult to prepare for problems such as sustaining progress and accepting benefits, but we must try.

The Issue

Imagination plays a role in emotional growth. You must anticipate obstacles and prepare for them, but you must also anticipate benefits. Obstacles generally take the form of resistance. Benefits generally come as surprises. There is no certainty with either, but it is foolish not to imagine the possibility of both.

Skills

People who struggle with depression, anxiety, and chronic stress tend to share a common trait. They don't trust anyone with their feelings. Of course the outcome of not trusting is the absence of feedback. One measure of emotional growth is increasing trust, which might mean a larger and more diverse support system, or it might mean a single mentor. In any case, skills that enhance trusting relationships are essential to emotional growth.

Goals

The goal of accepting benefits is entirely personal. It might come in the form of feelings that elevate the quality of your life, but it might take the form of cohesion within a group of people who share your values and methods. Or it might turn out that the goal of accepting benefits is spiritual; you appreciate the gifts you have been given and strive to thank the giver.

Summary

Emotional growth is multifaceted. You encounter it when you attend to your troubling feelings and particularly when you explore and express those feelings carefully so that you own them, even those that are not particularly comfortable.

You also encounter emotional growth when you choose to replace unwanted feelings that distort your perspective on the world with habits whose purpose is to restore perspective. This process calls for skills designed to restore perspective on the past, the future, and the present.

A third way emotional growth occurs is when we invest in our progress, that is, when we integrate perspective-building skills into our everyday lives and take responsibility for feelings such as hope, confidence, and peace of mind.

Thus we grow emotionally when we get grounded (chapter 2), when we choose to confront our unwanted feelings strategically (chapter 3), when we sustain our growth (chapter 4) and finally, when we accept its benefits (chapter 5). None of these options is the absolute right way, and none takes precedence over the others. Each of these pathways leads to something that enhances the quality of our emotional lives.

Exercises

Five Features of Emotional Growth

Instructions: Each of the following statements addresses a feature of emotional growth. Your response to each statement indicates a familiarity with the subject of this workbook. Explain your responses. Note the extent to which your responses change after you complete the book.

1. **Awareness of my troubling feelings**
   I occasionally feel depressed, anxious, or suffer from stress.   Yes___ No___

2. **Sharing my troubling feelings**
   When I feel depressed, anxious, or stressed, I ordinarily share my troubling feelings with someone who cares about me.   Yes___ No___

3. **Processing my troubling feelings**
   When I encounter troubling feelings, I tend to reflect on how I might have participated in my issue.   Yes___ No___

4. **Managing my emotional issue**
    I have the capacity to let go of my most painful losses, to be more assertive with my challenges, and to stay focused in times when things seem to be rapidly changing. Yes____ No____

5. **Learning from the process**
    My struggles with troubling feelings have helped me appreciate my personal gifts. Yes____ No____

Chapter 2

Getting Grounded

Introduction

When you are grounded, you acknowledge your troubling feelings as well as your participation in their development. You share them clearly and appropriately and refrain from blaming others or making excuses. You acknowledge your faults and take responsibility for them without apology. Thus, people who are grounded need not be admirable or even people of good character. So long as they own their feelings—all of them—they can be said to be grounded. This leaves lots of room for debate. Still, it seems safe to say that people who are grounded are in charge of their feelings, not the other way around.

Two questions are discussed in this chapter:

1. How do you get grounded?
2. What does it mean to take responsibility for your troubling feelings?

Skills for Getting Grounded

People who are grounded attend to their feelings, explore them, and express them (which is not the same as describing them as we shall see). Many readers probably already have some or all of these skills though they might not see them as skills or appreciate their utility.

The following diagram outlines the processing skills needed for becoming grounded.

Skills	Practice	Dynamic
Attending skills	Finding messages in troubling feelings	Separating issues from feelings
Exploring skills	Finding the history or context of troubling feelings	Owning participation in development of feelings
Expressing skills	Finding the meaning of troubling feelings	Distinguishing between describing and expressing feelings

Skills for Getting Grounded

Attending

When you think developmentally, you see troubling feelings as an early warning system. Like smoke alarms, they convey messages. The messages, however, are not warnings about what might happen in the physical world but about what might happen if you don't see past your feelings. Something in your processing is unresolved and needs further attention. Some examples are these.

- If you feel depressed, your feelings might reflect a loss that you have suffered but have not fully confronted. Depressive feelings tend to slow you down and draw you to the past. Rather than thinking of this process as a defect in your brain, consider the possibility that these feelings are subtle instructions to spend time becoming reconciled to your loss.

- When you feel anxious, you might feel muscle tension, pressure in your chest, or churning in your stomach. You might feel agitated by the limited choices you have, or you might feel vulnerable or even threatened by the looming challenges you face. In my case, public speaking invariably brings sweaty palms and an increased heart rate.

  Anxious feelings can be telling you that you are outside your comfort zone and need to ask for help. Or the message might be that you need to prepare plan B.

- Ordinary stress doesn't suggest that you reflect on your losses or prepare for unwanted challenges. It typically occurs in the course of your everyday life. But chronic stress is a different matter; it occurs when you experience a life transition.

  The problem with chronic stress is not that you are outside your comfort zone but that your comfort zone is not relevant to your new circumstances. The new realities are confusing. You aren't depressed or anxious; you are bewildered. Personal boundaries that once provided you with a sense of security are now useless. Competing priorities seem impossible to resolve.

When thinking developmentally, you understand that your troubling feelings provide you with information. The information is not straightforward or objective as is factual information that can be quantified, but it is nevertheless useful information.

Different troubling feelings deliver different messages, and as feelings become more intense or frequent, the demand for your attention becomes more urgent. The good news of emotional growth is that with practice and guidance, you can discern that information.

Exploring

Troubling feelings occur in a context. Many originated years or even decades ago. Exploring their history is called *contextualizing*. Some examples of contextualizing questions are these.

- When did I first have this feeling?
- What was going on in my life at that time?
- Who knew I had those feelings?
- Did they help me? How?

There are many others. Asking these questions helps you understand how your present feeling has evolved in the changing circumstances of your life. Suppose for example you contextualize your current depression. You start by noting that it started when your wife told you she wanted a divorce. You recollect that there was a breakdown in communication prior to her announcement, that solving family problems was often conflicted, and that you found reasons to be at work rather than at home. What did you do in response to her announcement? Whom did you confide in?

Did you seek marital or individual counseling? What did you feel on the occasion when the divorce was granted? And so on.

Contextualizing can be a painful process. I suspect that is why many people seek mental health counseling or the support of close friends to process this information. But the value of contextualizing far outweighs the temporary discomfort it creates. It forces you to see how you participated in the process that led to your current depressive feelings and ultimately to own those feelings.

Owning your troubling feelings is essential to becoming grounded. It is like taking out an insurance policy against feelings turning into issues. If you own your depressive feelings, you will be in charge of them; they will not be subject to the whims of another person or your biology. It's true that you had to pay a price for your ownership (you explored the history of unpleasant feelings), but that is a small price to pay compared to allowing others including medical professionals to have control of your feelings.

Of course, taking out insurance against depression, anxiety, and chronic stress is more complicated than buying "life insurance." Most of us tend to forget that we own our unwanted feelings. When that happens, we slip into blaming, resenting, and even becoming angry at the people or systems that we think caused our problems. Sometimes, staying grounded involves renewing our policies.

Expressing

It is important to distinguish between describing feelings and expressing them. Descriptions describe facts; they can be quantified. Thus, I might say that I sleep only about two hours at night and haven't talked with anyone all day. Or an anxious person might say that he can't relax due to constant muscle tension in his neck and shoulders, a throbbing headache, and an upset stomach. Descriptions of stress might be similar to those of anxiety, but they might also include experiences of momentary confusion or patterns of revisiting experiences.

Expressing feelings do not refer to facts. They make use of figurative language such as metaphors and similes. Expressive language is valuable because it is the language we ordinarily use to share our feelings with others who care about us. Consider the following examples.

- As a depressed person, you might express your pain by saying it is a burden or that it has recently grown heavier. You might say that you are stuck in a rut or that your grief feels raw as if it were an open wound. Some people admit to having dark moods; others simply say they feel blue. Others refer to weather to express their moods when they say that storm clouds are gathering.

- Anxious people might express their vulnerability by saying they are walking on egg shells or worry that they stand out like a sore thumb. More-severe anxiety might be expressed by saying you feel trapped between two unappealing choices or that you are walking on unsteady ground. Still more severe anxiety might be expressed in threatening metaphors such as walking along an abyss, falling, or waiting for the other shoe to drop.

- As a stressed person, it is likely that you are in the middle of a significant life transition, that something fundamental has disrupted your status quo. You might say that your life has been turned upside down, or that the changes in your life are moving at a rapid pace, or in more-severe cases, that things are spinning out of control.

It is useful to describe and then express your troubling feelings; the former provides a factual context that frequently is a diagnostic aid while the latter reveals both the scope of a person's feelings and its meaning.

The Advantage of Being Grounded

Being grounded doesn't mean you are without issues; rather, it means you go to the trouble of owning your troubling feelings. My experience with getting grounded occurred when I acknowledged my feelings about the absence of parental involvement during my later teen years. From age sixteen to twenty-two, I lived with relatives; during the little time I stayed with my family, they seemed to me to be strangers. Over a period of years, I recognized my feelings of abandonment first by exploring them in counseling and subsequently by expressing feelings of being set adrift, of constantly being out of my element, and of generally being a misfit.

But I was lucky. Lots of people helped me get ground. The work they did with me was like taking out an insurance policy. By assuming responsibility up front, I avoided the cost of repairs later on.

Taking Responsibility for your Feelings

Being responsible for your feelings means you recognize that you participated in their development. You might recognize that you relied too heavily on a coping technique and lost sight of your issue in the process. You might recognize that you are disposed to be drawn to the past and are therefore prone to depression. You might recognize that you simply lack the skills (such as those discussed in the next chapter) needed to restore perspective. But whatever you recognize in yourself is not a judgment of your character. Recognizing that you are a participant in the process is nothing more than an admission to being human. In any of the scenarios above, you make a statement about your functioning, not your character.

This is an important point. Pharmaceutical companies produce millions of brochures every year each one claiming that mental illnesses are diseases and that people who suffer from them bear no responsibility for their unfortunate condition. The suggestion that they do is thought to be evidence of stereotyping because it blames the victim for having symptoms over which he has no control. In fact, it does no such thing. Being responsible for troubling feelings makes you human.

Summary

People who are grounded own their emotional issues. They recognize messages, explore feelings, and use figurative language. However, being grounded is consistent with having troubling feelings. It is not an idealized state except in comparison with people who aren't grounded

Some people who aren't grounded realize that fact. They want to own their feelings but just don't know what steps to take. They don't know the skills they need, or perhaps they do but don't realize how to incorporate them into their daily lives. They haven't considered the possibility that getting grounded is a realistic and practical goal that offers many benefits.

Other people have no idea they aren't grounded; they are largely oblivious to their and others' feelings. They do not suffer from any particular emotional state; many of these people lead satisfying lives moving from one problem-solving episode to another. These people, however, are susceptible to more-complicated struggles in the event that circumstances force them to deal with the reality of their troubling feelings.

The best outcome for being grounded is self-knowledge

Exercises

If you can talk about your feelings, you can control them. If you can't, they are likely to control you.

Attending Skills

Describe a troubling feeling that dominates or is pervasive in your emotional life. Does this feeling draw you to the past? Does it create doubt in your ability? Or does it leave you feeling aimless and confused? Remember: your job here is to understand your feeling, not to resolve it.

Contextualizing Skills

Select a feeling you have struggled with and answer the following questions.

1. What do you first remember having this feeling?
2. What was happening in your life at that time?
3. Was the key event a loss, an uncertain period in your life, or a transition?
4. Who knew about this event? Was it a secret?
5. Did the people who knew about the event try to help you? Did they actually help you?
6. Did you seek professional help? Did you counseling or some other kind of guidance?
7. How has the feeling you are describing changed since you first noticed it?

What issues do you patterns suggest? For instance, were you passive or assertive, receptive to offers of help, or defensive? Were you able to compartmentalize your struggle, or did it alter your life in significant ways? Remember: you are telling a story, your story. There are no right answers.

Expressive and Descriptive Skills

Describe a feeling you have frequently using the following terminology.

1. muscle tension
2. headaches
3. upset stomach
4. disrupted sleep patterns
5. irritability
6. mood swings
7. loss of appetite

Use the following terminology to express that same feeling. If you aren't accustomed to figurative language, just do your best.

My feeling is

1. a burden
2. an injury or a wound
3. pressure I can hardly contain
4. so disconcerting that I feel lost
5. so disruptive that I feel broken
6. so debilitating that I feel stuck
7. so realistic that I feel I'm in danger

There are many variations of these examples. Give any examples that express your particular feeling.

Suppose you are talking to a good friend and want to tell him about the troubling feelings you've been having. Would you use literal language, figurative language, or both? Explain.

Chapter 3

Perspective

Introduction

This chapter provides a sketch of the role of perspective and the consequences of losing perspective.

Perspective is the lens through which you interpret experiences in the world. Most of our adult experiences are routine; we solve problems about what to do next. These problems are shaped by our relationships, jobs, values, and interests. Occasionally however, we encounter difficult experiences. The patterns we have established do not offer clear paths. These difficult experiences tend to occur when we suffer a loss, when we confront challenges that create self-doubt, and when we find ourselves in the middle of one of life's inevitable transitions. These difficult experiences generate troubling feelings. In general, losses generate depressive feelings, challenges generate anxious feelings, and life transitions generate stress.

In spite of the fact that troubling feelings are at the very least uncomfortable, they are also opportunities to think of a troubling feeling as a messenger. It conveys information about your perspective. So depressive feelings might draw you into the past, to dwell on a particular loss, and perhaps to allow it to take hold of your imagination. Likewise, anxious feelings might create an aversion to the future, of the unknown, and if allowed to fester, it might be the basis of dread. And chronic stress might signal that you are out of your comfort zone, that what had previously been relaxing is no longer that. In short, you can learn from your troubling feelings not about the world of facts outside but the world within.

Perspective is not a mechanism located somewhere in the human body and so it is not quantifiable. It is in other words a useless concept to advocates of the medical model but essential to advocates of emotional growth. Without perspective, there is no emotional growth.

Advocates of the medical model insist that key concepts be quantifiable; they have no use for perspective. For them, troubling feelings are symptoms of biological defects and nothing more. Advocates of emotional growth on the other hand embrace the role of perspective. It explains a common human experience: the capacity to reflect on troubling feelings and recognize their meaning. You might not grasp the full extent of their meaning, but if you think developmentally, you will look beyond the feeling for its message. The message might not be neat and tidy such as facts are supposed to be, but it lets you know that you have these feelings for a reason. They inform you about how you interpret difficult experiences.

Coping Skills

Everyone has some coping skills. Without them, our lives would be awful. The capacity to suppress emotional pain, postpone an untimely demand, or rationalize an unexpected consequence is part of living in a complicated world. Coping skills provide relief from setbacks, disappointments, dread, confusion, and many other difficulties we encounter. In fact, as the diagram below illustrates, coping skills have limited effectiveness. Think of them as your personal first responders.

Skills	Circumstances	Limits
Suppression	Dealing with grief and other major losses	Neglect of the issue of loss
Avoidance	Dealing with perceived threats and vulnerabilities	Neglect of challenges underlying the unwanted feelings
Rationalizing	Dealing with life transitions	Neglect of the reality of existing changes
Masking	Dealing with feelings of inadequacy	Neglect of generalized unwanted feelings
Humor	Dealing with rejection and disappointment	Neglect of issues of loss
Exercise	Dealing with anger and frustration	Neglect of self-care

Coping Skills

Suppression

We tend to suppress losses and especially significant losses that are too difficult to process. Suppression is useful because it allows us to process such losses over time so that the impact of the loss can be managed. Funerals for example allow us to postpone dealing with grief until we are in the company of people who share our grief.

Avoiding or Deflecting

When we face an unpleasant task, we are tempted to postpone it. Personal examples include my annual meeting with my CPA to do my taxes and any occasion that calls for public speaking. When I face chores around the house, I find that a trip to the gym is absolutely necessary. Even so, avoiding can be practical if you buy time to prepare for the chore in question.

Rationalization

We tend to rationalize when change disrupts our routines. Moving to a new home or having your children move out of your home can be very stressful; in such situations, people rationalize the matter and tell themselves that nothing important will change in spite of the change at hand. This of course is not true, but it is a comforting thought that eases the transition to a new reality.

Masking and Denial

Denial is a blunt instrument; it allows us to simply refuse to acknowledge unwanted feelings. Even when confronted with evidence that they are suffering, some people simply reiterate their denials sometimes with increasing hostility.

Masking is like denial except that it makes use of alcohol and drugs. When you mask your feelings, it is superficially true that they don't exist, but that is only because you have used chemicals to support your denials.

Humor

Humor seems like an odd coping skill, but it is widely used. Many comedians report that they use comedy to process the difficulties they encountered in their youth. Some people laugh at their own foibles. Some use sarcasm; after a misfortune, someone might ask a friend, "Don't you envy me?" Some remark on the irony of how rapidly their fortunes change; they might say, "I was doing really well until the wheels came off."

Exercise

Exercise is a remarkably effective coping tool. Whether by jogging, training for a marathon, yoga classes, or mountain climbing, many people have found exercise allows them to set aside their misery for a short time and transfer their misery into motivation.

Losing Perspective

Another feature of losing perspective is that it is pervasive. The diagram below illustrates the many ways you can become aware that you have lost perspective.

Baseline	Losing perspective on the past	Losing perspective on the future	Losing perspective on the present
I cope by …	Suppressing and denying depressive feelings.	Avoiding, deflecting, and medicating anxious feelings	Rationalizing and conforming to new norms to mediate chronic stress
I struggle with …	Letting go. My losses dominate my daily functioning.	Being assertive. Self-doubt dominates my daily functioning.	Staying focused. I can't concentrate on anything.
I am …	A victim. I can't escape my past.	A loser. I can't deal with the uncertainty in my life.	An outsider. I can't adjust to the major transitions in my life.
I feel …	Hopeless. I am defined by my losses.	Helpless. I am defined by my limitations.	Overwhelmed. I am defined by my circumstances.

Losing Perspective

Losing perspective is a common phenomenon. We use coping skills to mediate troubling feelings all the time without thinking about it. When we do, we alter our interpretation of the world to a degree, but the trade-off is part of the bargain. We give up a bit of objectivity for relief from emotional pain. Sometimes, we do so knowingly as when we defer dealing with grief until a funeral when we will be supported by others who share our grief. Sometimes, we do so unwittingly as when we tell ourselves lies about how nothing will change after our children move away from our care.

For the most part, losing perspective is of little significance. The bargain we make with ourselves is short term. We work out our grief by gradually replacing the loss with something else we value. We recognize that our rationalizations have a short shelf life either because our support system makes us aware of the deception or because we simply recognize the reality of the life transition on our own.

In any event, within limits, using coping techniques creates no particular problems. However, problems always arise when they are overused. If you suppress grief not as a coping technique but as a strategy for dealing with a significant loss, you will never deal with your long-term issue. There is irony in emotional growth. The same techniques that produce great comfort in the short term block long-term growth.

I have tried to avoid technical terms in this workbook; it is important to use some terms with care. Thus, coping applies to feelings whereas managing applies to issues. The difference lies in the fact that coping skills are responses (first responders) while managing is strategic. We cope more or less automatically, but we need goals and plans to manage our long-term issues with loss, self-doubt, and lack of focus. Still, they are related ideas. If we cope effectively and appropriately with our troubling feelings, they most likely won't develop into issues, but if we overextend our coping skills, chances are that we will encounter emotional issues.

Consider another example. Suppose your pattern is to postpone, avoid, or deflect, i.e., to choose a frivolous or less demanding activity. You might have used these techniques to buy time, to regroup, or simply to relax. But if postponing unpleasant chores becomes a habit or if you fail to use the time gained wisely, postponing handling problems can turn them into catastrophes. The coping tool that served you well becomes woefully inadequate as a long-term strategy.

The Consequence of Losing Perspective

The consequence of diminished perspective is that your struggles intensify. If you suppress depressive feelings too long, sorrow becomes a habit and then perhaps turns into an obsession. Instead of dissipating, your feelings take on a life of their own. Since you have suppressed your feelings, most of that life is beneath the surface, but the consequence is that after a while, you can't let go and your depressive feelings turn into depression.

Anxiety follows a similar script. If you postpone, deflect, and otherwise procrastinate with a particularly onerous challenge, your coping becomes habitual and possibly automatic. Your anxiety turns into self-doubt, and if it is allowed to continue, you can become immobilized. Loss of perspective on the future in whatever form it takes erodes confidence.

Chronic stress might start with simple social awkwardness. Any life transition is likely to be stressful. If, however, rationalizing the reality of changing circumstances is your only coping tool and you persist in using it long after a reasonable adjustment period, your grasp of the transition is compromised; you start believing the fantasy that nothing has changed, and pretty soon, you start believing that nothing will change, a dangerous outcome to a coping skill that starts out quite innocently.

In short, using coping skills beyond their short-term purposes is a setup for emotional distress of all kinds. Of course, these limits are inexact and cannot be quantified. Thus, though this account has no place in the medical model, it is the basis for claiming that emotional growth is an optimistic approach to mental health issues because even though we sometimes adopt dysfunctional habits that diminish our perspective, we can also adopt purposeful habits that restore perspective. There is nothing that forces us to choose dysfunctional habits or to cling to them; when we do, there is nothing that says we can't restore our perspective, at least not in the emotional growth approach.

Advantages of the Developmental Model

At the outset this workbook claimed to be an alternative to the medical model. It offers a view that is developmental. That is, emotional issues are consequences of how you process troubling feelings. If you don't attend to your feelings, you never learn to own them and thus don't recognize your role in their development.

If you cope with them but allow coping to become habitual, you don't recognize that troubling feelings are not emotional issues and therefore lose sight of the fact that you can act purposefully to find relief. In either case, emotional issues are not caused by biological defects; in fact, biology facts play no role in the understanding of depression, anxiety, and chronic stress.

This conclusion is for many a radical departure from mainstream mental health thinking. My purpose is not to argue with advocates of the medical model other than to note that the model's hypothesis is that troubling feelings are symptoms of and therefore caused by physical states in the brain. My purpose is to make the developmental model as credible as I can. With that in mind, I propose the following as working definitions of depression, anxiety, and chronic stress.

- Depression is diminished perspective on the past such that you feel that the past dominates your current functioning. It is characterized by a struggle to let go of a particular loss. Evidence of depression is often found in the language used to express feelings. Full-blown depression occurs when you believe the future will always repeat past patterns resulting in a sense of hopeless.

- Anxiety is diminished perspective on the future such that you feel your options have narrowed and you become increasingly less assertive. It is characterized by a sense of self-doubt and aversion to new challenges. Further evidence is found in expressive language used by anxious people indicating that they feel threatened or trapped by no-win options. Full-blown anxiety occurs when you believe your choices have no bearing on events resulting in a sense of helplessness.

- Chronic stress is diminished perspective on the present such that you feel confused or disoriented in your present circumstances. It is characterized by an inability to stay focused and relax. It typically occurs during life transitions involving changes in family structure, moving, and even career changes. Evidence of chronic stress is often noted in expressions used by the stressed person. Full-blown stress occurs when the pace of events in your life is so overwhelming that it erodes your quality of life.

Developmental definitions describe the process of becoming depressed, anxious, and chronically stressed and by extension the condition of being depressed, anxious, and chronically stressed. These definitions have two advantages over medical ones.

1. Developmental definitions are more accessible to ordinary people than medical diagnoses are. Mental health issues are identified in terms of the loss of perspective that is reflected in your orientation to the past, the future, or the present and hence make no reference to their causes.
2. Developmental definitions address prevention of mental illnesses whereas medical definitions are limited to the treatment of such conditions after they are established.

Summary

The core of emotional growth is this: troubling feelings are normal human experiences. Many of the techniques we use to cope with them are generally effective with unwanted feelings but not with issues such as loss, self-doubt, and lack of focus. Being human, we are prone to take care of our feelings first and hence to rely on our coping skills.

The consequence of this approach is that we often neglect our capacity to learn skills that deal with emotional issues which tend to grow when neglected.

Thus, our issues with depression, anxiety, and chronic stress are unintended consequence of our human frailty. We don't intend to become depressed, but being human, we tend to our depressive feelings even though doing so often exacerbates our struggle. In a developmental sense, mental illnesses are not a characteristic of physical defects, genetic predispositions, or anything else that can be quantified; they are a characteristic of our fallible nature.

We need to expand the public understanding of emotional growth and provide systems that facilitate guidance. The remaining chapters discusses the matter of restoring perspective, sustaining the progress we make, and developing a notion about the benefits of emotional growth in the first place. These ideas are the basis of guidance for anyone who takes emotional issues seriously.

Exercises

Coping Skills
Check the responses that best describe you.
In general, when coping with troubling feelings, do you

1. Withdraw emotionally? _____
2. Isolate yourself? _____
3. Become angry or defensive? _____
4. Become submissive? _____
5. Suppress your feelings? _____
6. Use drugs and/or alcohol? _____
7. Become pessimistic or fatalistic? _____
8. Act impulsively? _____
9. Use humor or sarcasm? _____

Provide details that illustrate your responses.

Select one of the following scenarios and discuss how your coping and processing skills (or lack of them) have contributed to your unwanted feelings.

Scenario 1: I've become discouraged.
Being discouraged is a normal part of life, but it can also be a sign of losing perspective on the past.

Scenario 2: I worry about everything.
Worry that leads to an action plan is healthy, but if you worry obsessively, you risk becoming immobilized.

Scenario 3: I'm not focused.
When you are stressed, it is difficult to concentrate on important tasks and even more difficult to prioritize the tasks you need to do. You are likely to be easily distracted.

Scenario 4: I don't trust anyone.
If you have a history of depression, anxiety, or stress, you probably find that trusting others is difficult.

Exercises
Questions

1. What troubling feeling do those skills help you cope with? For instance, did you suppress a loss, rationalize a change, or deflect a difficult decision?
2. Which of your coping skills were most effective? Which was least effective?

Chapter 4

Restoring Perspective

Introduction

Losing perspective is easy. We do it all the time. All we need to do is ignore the messages conveyed by our troubling feelings and cling to our favorite coping devices rather than identifying and confronting the issues they represent. But most of us are fortunate enough to have adequate resources or support systems that protect us from permanent damage. At any rate, we don't rely on coping techniques as long-term strategies for finding relief.

If life were fair, restoring perspective would be as easy as losing it, but of course it isn't. For starters, restoring perspective doesn't change the facts you struggle with; it changes what you are willing to do about those facts. To restore perspective—to build a solid structure—you need three elements.

1. Goals that motivate you to act
2. Strategies that translate your goals into a system of specific objectives
3. Skills that you implement to achieve your objectives

The emotional growth diagram below suggests goals, strategies, and skills designed to promote emotional growth.

The remainder of this chapter describes some key skills needed to restore perspective on the past, future, and present (see the Losing Perspective Diagram on page 26). It is important to note that the emotional growth approach is a developmental definition. As such, it addresses not only depression, anxiety, and chronic stress but also the prevention of these conditions as well. The question is not, how can we treat mood disorders after they have become firmly entrenched? but rather, How can we identify signs of losing perspective and take steps to restore perspective? This second question is not technically a mental health question if mental health is defined as treatment of entrenched habits caused by biological or genetic states. It is, however, a question whose answer will empower people who struggle with depressive, anxious, and chronically stressful feelings.

A Framework for Restoring Perspective

Suppose you struggle with a tangled mess of unwanted feelings. Also, suppose you have tried everything including conventional mental health counseling, various prescribed medications, an assortment of self-help schemes (light boxes, magnets, meditation, and so forth) but still have not found the relief you were seeking. In addition, you practice reasonable self-care habits—you eat well, sleep well, work, and have a few social outlets. Still, you struggle with depressive or anxious feelings or way too much stress.

The reality is that though you might have tried many conventional approaches, you haven't had the opportunity to think developmentally. The key elements of thinking developmentally are as follows

- I participated in the development of my troubling feelings.
- I can understand how I participated.
- I can change my perspective by adopting purposeful goals and realistic strategies.
- I can enhance the quality of my emotional life.

The message you articulate is, I got myself into this mess, and so I can jolly well get myself out of it. I'm certain I'll need guidance and emotional support, but it is up to me to take care of business. With that in mind, the diagram below is offered as a framework for people who are prepared to take responsibility for their feelings.

	Goals	**Strategies**	**Skill 1**	**Skill 2**
Past	Emotional distance	Change the meaning of your losses	Reframing so that losses have value	Refocusing
Future	Assertiveness	Formulate challenges as discrete projects	Projects that structure the future	Action plans that formalize projects
Present	Focus	Staying in the present moment	Mindfulness	Playfulness, Affirmations

Restoring Perspective

Restoring Perspective on the Past

The key to restoring perspective on the past is strategic: to acknowledge the facts associated with your loss as permanent but to change the meaning of those facts. This is hard work that often requires sensitive emotional support and sometimes professional mental health counseling.

Suppose the facts you must deal with are something like the following.

- Yes, my wife left me for another man.
- Yes, I was fired for sticking to my principles.
- Yes, my child died in a needless traffic accident.
- Yes, I have been diagnosed with inoperable cancer.

Reframing

These are clearly depressing facts. It is easy to see how those dealing with one of these situations might feel like a victim. It is also easy to understand that they desire to let go of their losses. They can deny the facts or they can reinterpret their meaning. Using a technical term, they can reframe them. There are many way to reframe a loss. Among them are the following.

- You can celebrate some losses by recognizing the contributions made by the person lost. Many funerals are exercises in reframing. You can also initiate campaigns in the name of a deceased person as a way of remembering them.

- You can join a group of people who have suffered similar losses thereby meeting people who have explored the depth of the loss that is still new to you.

- You can reframe your loss in terms of lessons learned. A bitter divorce might make you aware of your failure to communicate feelings clearly and directly. Some people feel that their divorce transformed them, and after a painful process, they appreciate their failed marriages in a radically new light.

Reframing is not easy. It typically follows periods of denial, anger, and confusion. Many people need intensive emotional support and lots of active listening; others need professional counseling to get through the process. But the point is that you can reframe most of your losses. You can let go of the view that you are a victim and replace it with a view that in spite of your loss and possibly because of it, you have learned something important about yourself and perhaps have uncovered a deeper sense of community.

When you reframe a loss, it loses its grip on your perspective. You see the past not as an immutable fixture that necessarily dominates your current life but as real though painful events that occurred that you can reinterpret. Their meaning for your current life changes when you change your perspective. You can keep the memory of your loss but let go of the pain associated with it.

Refocusing

Many people need help with reframing, and some need professional help. Some can't. The loss they feel is so intense or vast that it is impossible for them to find the slightest silver lining. What can be done for these people?

Refocusing is a thought experiment that uses imagination. Suppose you temporarily suspend your emotional pain. You don't deny it or suppress it, and it is understood that you can't reframe it. While suspending your pain, you focus on some long-term want. It might be anything from some wild fantasy to something you imagine will fill your life with meaning.

Since this is a thought experiment, you don't worry about how to make this fantasy become real. Refocusing is simply a tool for finding respite from the grind of grappling with your loss. It puts you in touch with other feelings you might have not felt in a long time. It is a little like taking a trial separation in a problem marriage. When the period of refocusing is over, you can return to the status quo. Chances are that things won't change all at once, but if you work at it, they might.

Building Perspective on the Future

Anxiety thrives in the absence of structure. Some people feel anxious when they face a day with nothing to do. Some struggle to get out of bed because their lives feel empty. Some people live one day at a time because the structure in their lives is uncertain. Their jobs, marriages, and important relationships are unstable. Deadlines loom large, confrontations are threatening, and seemingly insignificant comments take on a life of their own. In the absence of structure, they feel anxious.

Some anxiety stems from too much structure or structure that draws you out of your comfort zone. This kind of anxiety puts you on the defense; you feel you must prove your competence to complete a task or confront a hostile encounter. The anxiety addressed in this workbook, however, arises from an uncertain future or more likely being in a situation in which roles are so poorly defined that there are no performance standards. Your job is to be assertive, to create structures, or to design projects.

Projects

You restore perspective on the future by selecting projects that get you out of your comfort zone but only a short distance away. If you are anxious about public speaking, you might design a project that involves reading in front of a mirror until that seems easy, and then going on to reading in front of a friend who might give you feedback.

If you are anxious about going to public places, you might design a project in which you take walks in the early morning when there is little chance of encountering anyone, and after that feels comfortable, asking a friend to walk with you.

If you are anxious about having a difficult conversation with a significant other, you could imagine scenarios and practice them with a trusted friend. There is no project too small to lure you out of your comfort zone though projects are not always easy to design.

Of course some projects are more complicated than the ones mentioned in the paragraphs above. If the source of your anxiety is a performance of some kind, the only project that makes sense is practicing it. If the source is to meet a deadline, your project would be to ask for help or perhaps ask someone to give supportive feedback. In any event, the idea here is to reduce daunting challenges to small components and then select the simplest part for your initial project.

Designing projects requires a certain amount of creativity. Time constraints do not always allow for this technique, but being assertive is an option that is often overlooked by people who suffer with anxiety. As is the case with reframing, you might need professional help, but building a structured future out of simple projects is a powerful tool.

Action Plans

Projects are by definition informal. However, there is nothing that prevents you from cultivating a more formal project by adopting an action plan with goals, objectives, timetables, contingency plans, and so forth.

Building Perspective on the Present

The present is a paradox; it is permanently present but always fleeting. How can you not be in the present moment? But how can you occupy something that is forever disappearing?

We are generally aware of the passage of time. We get to work on time, keep our appointments on time, and track how much time is on the clock during football and basketball games. Our spouses sometimes want to know what time they should expect us when we go out. For the most part, we measure our time by the clock.

But at other times, we are oblivious to the passage of time. We might be enjoying a sunset or entertaining a two-year-old who actually laughs at our jokes. We might be so caught up in work that time gets away from us. Or we might simply be in a playful mood, enjoying the company of others and our own silliness. On such occasions, time seems to stand still. We are refreshed and energized by such experiences.

Perhaps, then, time is not a paradox but is shaped by skills that allow us to focus our attention on the immediacy of what we are doing. We need to have a closer look at some of those skills.

Mindfulness

When you are being mindful, you attend to your senses—what you hear, see, smell, touch, and taste without interpretation. A cloud isn't a cloud but an irregularly shaped set of white and grey forms moving gradually overhead. Taking a walk in the park, you might note warmth on your skin, a cooling breeze, chirping sounds, and the arc of a hawk in flight.

Or you might note the churning in your stomach, the throbbing pain in your left knee, the tension in your neck, or the relaxed feeling that comes with a warm cup of coffee. In any event, whenever you are attending to the immediate nature of your experience without judgment or interpretation, you are engaged in the present. You are mindful that you aren't problem solving, judging the worth of something, analyzing a problem, or interpreting the meaning of the things; you are simply attending to your senses—nothing more.

Mindfulness is a skill that requires practice. Many people learn it in formal settings, but there is nothing about mindfulness that requires formal instruction. If you can be attentive to your feelings and senses without judging them or dismissing your thoughts as random distractions and embrace the naturalness of the exercise, you can be mindful. Nevertheless, many people benefit from instruction on how to be mindful.

Mindfulness provides an alternative to getting caught in the confusion and turmoil of daily life. It is not an escape from reality; rather, it is attending to a reality that enhances the quality of life for those who take the time to learn the skill of being mindful.

You can be mindful without knowing it. Consider noncompetitive play. You can play with another person not to solve a problem or gain an advantage over him or her but simply for the sheer joy of it. If you have ever thrown a Frisbee for an eager-to-please dog, you have been mindful. If you have made small talk with a stranger, you have been mindful. My favorite way of being mindful is engaging in random banter with a youngster. These activities have no purpose other than mutual enjoyment.

There are many variations on the theme of staying present. It is the simplest of skills and yet the least used at least in modern industrial societies.

Playfulness

Playfulness is completely unnecessary; it serves no specific purpose and solves no problems. You play for the fun of it. What is happening in the present moment is all that matters; you are for a moment indifferent to what has happened or what might happen. The passage of time as measured by clocks is irrelevant. However, playfulness itself has a purpose—it removes you from the world that is measured by clocks. Like mindfulness, it is a stress reducer.

There are lots of ways to be playful. You can be playful with your dog, a two-year-old, or with friends. You can be playful while making small talk with strangers, a waiter, or your dentist. Playfulness is mutual; when you are playful, you share a moment of mutual mindfulness with another person or another playful being such as a dog.

How can you learn to be playful? If you are shy, you can practice small talk while standing in a slow-moving line. You tell yourself that it doesn't matter what you say because you will never see the other person again, so you can ask a stranger an open-ended question or make an observation about anything. You might even offer a compliment if you are feeling brave. You might be ignored, but if you get a response, you have started a conversation; your job is to keep it going for a minute or two and then close it cheerfully. If you take the initiative, you can learn to be playful.

In the end, playfulness is serious business; it teaches you how to bond and feel good about another person; eventually, it is a component of intimacy.

Self-Affirmations

I have a problem with self-affirmations; they make me feel awkward, as if I'm congratulating myself. If I do so publicly, I'm certain someone who hears me will correct me and probably say something to show that my claim wasn't warranted. For me, self-affirmation is a skill that needs to be practiced. I'm still not sure I have gotten it right.

The first step is learning the vocabulary of self-affirmations. Some examples are below.

- I didn't think I could do that, but I did!
- Not a bad job even if I do say so myself.
- I surprised myself.
- I didn't get the job done, but I made a great effort.
- I don't know anyone who could have done a better job than I did.

The second step is to cultivate a habit of affirming yourself each morning the moment your feet touch the floor. Another skill is to refrain from making self-effacing comments. Yet another is to include others in your affirmation. You often want to note the group's efforts and not single out yourself.

Summary

Though many mainstream mental health professionals would argue that emotional growth stigmatizes the mentally ill by the mere mention of responsibility, the reality is that acknowledging responsibility is liberating. It suggests that even though you struggle with unwanted feelings, you have the capacity to restore your perspective. You can reframe, design projects and action plans, be mindful, and discover other ways to stay in the present. You can learn these skills; you might already possess them but not know that they can be applied to replace troubling feelings with productive ones. Any view that suggests you can't learn and apply these skills to the practical problems of life seems to me to stigmatize the mentally ill.

Restoring perspective might sound easy to people who have never done it. All you need to do, it seems to them, is discard old dysfunctional habits and make rational choices to replace them with more functional habits. However, restoring perspective is only possible when you understand how you participated in the process of losing perspective in the first place how to select goals that take your attention from feelings to issues. Restoring perspective is a process of thinking developmentally about troubling feelings, what they mean, and what you can do to find relief from them.

The next chapter is not so much finding relief as it is sustaining it.

Exercises

Restoring Perspective on the Past: *Can you let go of significant losses?*

Reframing

- Describe what was lost and the context in which it was lost.
- Describe your initial feelings about what you lost. What did it mean to you? Did you feel humiliated, victimized, stuck, or hopeless about your prospects?

Exercises

- Look back on the meaning of your loss. Did your loss present you with new opportunities, allow you to share feelings with people who identify with your loss, lead to feelings of gratitude for good memories, or enhance your awareness of how you participated in the loss so that you were able to make relevant changes? Explain.

- Reflect on the reframing process. What was the process like for you? Did you have help? Are you settled, or do you continue to work on reframing? Explain.

Restoring Perspective on the Future: *Can you be more assertive?*

Design a Project

- Describe the challenge you face.
- Describe your feelings about the challenge. Do you feel trapped by unappealing choices, inadequate to do what is expected of you, isolated, and intimidated?
- What does this challenge mean to you? Does it reflect on your character? Are you concerned with what your friends might think of you, or is competence your main concern?

Design a Project for Your Current Challenge

Design a project for one of the following scenarios

- You have been terminated from a job you enjoyed. Now you face a day with nothing to do.
- You are invited to be a guest speaker at a civic organization in your community. You are competent in your field but not a good public speaker.
- You are agoraphobic. The idea of being in public places is terrifying.

Restoring Perspective on the Present: *Can you stay focused?*

Staying Present

- Describe the life transition you have encountered.
- Describe your feelings. For instance, do you feel vulnerable, confused, excluded? Do you feel you are an outsider?
- What is the meaning of this experience? Do you believe you've lost the ability to concentrate or that your brain is somehow impaired?

Being Mindful

- Start by attending to all the sensations you have as you sit in a comfortable chair. Note the colors, shapes, textures, sounds, aromas, and sounds you experience while resting quietly. Do not draw any conclusions or make any judgments about your observations. Do this twice daily.
- An alternative exercise is to attend to the sensations you feel while resting. Note the tension of your muscles, throbbing of your heart, growling in your stomach, itches, aches, and pains. If thoughts interrupt the exercise, make a note of the thoughts you have as if you are an observer and return to the exercise. Again, do not draw conclusions or make judgments about your observations.
- These exercises will probably feel strange at first, but your job in doing these exercises is to practice mindfulness, not to solve or analyze problems.

Being Playful

- Start by initiating a conversation with a stranger while standing in line to make a purchase or ordering food at a fast-food restaurant. Alternatively, if you have a pet, play with it; if you happen to be in contact with parents of an infant, talk to the infant, or if you are in contact with youngsters, ask them open-ended questions about their interests. The idea is to be in unstructured situation where the interaction is an end in itself.

- Play a role in adult conversation in which you represent a position that you can defend but don't actually support. Be as convincing as possible. It's a game.

- Find opportunities to be silly, to be the butt of your own joke, to laugh at jokes made by others, or best of all, to make puns. The idea is to not take yourself so seriously.

Being Affirmative

- Start by noting a successful outcome; it doesn't need to be a major accomplishment. It is enough to note a day in which you were mindful twice or had a playful experience. Do not be deterred by others who are critical of you for taking undeserved credit. You lose the effect of the affirmation if you allow others to diminish it.

- Affirm someone else who made progress toward a specific project. Note that an affirmation is not a compliment. Affirmations are words of encouragement; compliments are intended to be flattering.

- Recommitting yourself to goals is a kind of affirmation.

Chapter 5

Sustaining Perspective

Introduction

It is one thing to practice a skill under controlled conditions but quite another to use it in a world that is indifferent to your well-being. To sustain emotional growth, you need to prepare for the latter. Two elements are critically important.

1. Anticipate all kinds of obstacles the most significant being your resistance to change. Resistance always seems to be lurking under the surface.
2. Take care of your physical, social, and spiritual self. The hard part of self-care is oddly learning how to trust and whom to trust.

Anticipate Resistance

The most predictable obstacle to emotional growth is your resistance to change. Resistance occurs when your brain tells you to work on your goals but your muscles aren't accustomed to the exercise. It comes in many forms, and some of them are quite subtle.

Minimizing and Discounting

We minimize our progress when we say, "It's no big deal," and we discount it when we compare ourselves unfavorably to others. Statements such as "Anyone could have done that" or "It's about time I got something right" are examples of discounting and minimizing. Comments such as these undermine recovery. They acknowledge that perspective was restored. Perhaps you were able to reframe an important loss, but then, instead of accepting the fact that you had made progress, you criticize yourself for not having made more progress or for not having made the progress sooner.

Perhaps you were able to devise an action plan but then decided that your project was of no great significance or that you could just as well have learned to be more assertive in another way. In either case, you criticize yourself for having held onto it for such a long time. Instead of integrating your progress, you criticize yourself by minimizing your ability to reframe or discounting your initiative to be assertive.

Minimizing and discounting are subtle and devious weapons that often masquerade as modesty. Modesty is a covert technique that allows you to maintain old habits, and the appeal of old habits is that though they are associated with misery and pain; they spare you the trouble of redefining yourself. The real obstacle to recovery here is that old, familiar patterns often seem preferable to new, risky ones, and so, many people give up their recovery programs.

Self-deprecating comments then are the enemy of emotional growth. To combat such obstacles, you need a lively and diverse support system that confronts your ploys to retreat and allows you to take comfort in your depression, anxiety, or chronic stress.

Rigidity

Rigidity is based on the assumption that there is only one strategy for any goal. If the strategy doesn't yield the desired results quickly, the entire project is considered flawed. Clearly, this is not a mind-set conducive to recovery. Recovery calls for flexibility and a willingness to try other possibilities. The goal might be to expand your social horizon by going to the library once a week. But if the only way to get to the library is by taking a bus and the bus schedule changes, you need to adjust your plan, not toss it out.

When we launch a new project, we risk being naive, overly ambitious, or simply ignorant of some critical facts. This is especially true when we are trying to be self-reliant. Our chances of success increase when we seek others who care about us and have experience that we lack. But some people who engage in recovery are stubborn; they don't want to trouble anyone else with their struggles. These people need to be aware of the dangers of too much rugged individualism.

Rigidity pretends to be principled. If you are working on a recovery project but are too rigid, you might tell yourself that a setback is evidence of a flawed plan and hence evidence of a flawed person; you didn't get the plan right, so you can't get the plan right. This kind of thinking gives you permission to feel bad, unworthy, or simply incompetent. In any event, it erodes initiative. Why try to apply new skills if you aren't able to devise a workable plan?

Perfectionism

Perfectionism is the downfall of many recovery plans. Like minimizing and discounting, it is self-inflicted, but instead of being self-deprecating, it is self-inflating. Ordinary standards aren't good enough for perfectionists; their standards are superior, their goals are elevated, and their strategies are sure to bring the desired outcomes.

Perfectionists are rigid but with a twist. Other strategies might be good enough for others but not for them. By insisting on perfection, they mask their humanity behind a façade of idealism. They are better because their standards are better. Of course, when they don't achieve a desired outcome, they have excuses at the ready—failure is due to elevated standards, not their lack of commitment.

Perfectionism disguises itself as a lack of commitment. Perfectionists identify with idealistic goals and select strategies that are unrealistic if not impossible to put into play. They say in effect, "I didn't achieve my goal not because I didn't try but because my standards are so high." Idealistic goals are a recipe for personal failure.

Recovery calls for a vision, not a fantasy. Lofty ideals might feel and sound good, but they don't make for solid action plans. A vision on the other hand is grounded not in what you say but in what you do. It mixes goals that pull you into the future with tasks that constantly push you out of your comfort zone.

Unhealthy Comparisons

Minimizing, discounting, and being rigid and perfectionist block recovery or for some people emotional growth. They are ploys used by many recovering people to return to the comfort of old habits rather than risk the unknown territory of self-discovery. Together, they indicate how difficult recovery can be. We don't need modern science to explain the reoccurrence of emotional issues, a common phenomenon in recovery. The developmental approach explains it easily in nonmedical terms.

In fact, resistance to recovery runs even deeper. I have my own experience as an example. I seldom get things right the first time. I have a history of computer mistakes to prove my point. As I compound my mistakes, I get discouraged and frustrated. Like most people, I hate to seek assistance; doing so makes me feel inferior and stupid. Instead, I compare myself to others who are novices as I am but who can seemingly work through the hazards of computer technology. By comparing myself in this way, I lose interest in my project and compound my frustration.

If you compare yourself unfavorably to anyone, your recovery program is certain to suffer a setback.

Overcoming Resistance

When you anticipate resistance, you have already done most of the work of overcoming it. What remains is to select plan B, which can allow you to be flexible and to adjust to unforeseen realities without feeling a failure because your original plan didn't work out.

The feeling that you have failed is the demise of many emotional growth programs; negative self-talk gives you permission to be cynical—"See? I told you couldn't do it." If you minimize pain, you give yourself permission to suppress. If you become rigid, you make it impossible to formulate an action plan. If you insist on being perfect—perhaps the most common obstacle—you are planning on failure.

Asking for Help

Another response is to ask for help. Part of restoring perspective is trust. You might be rejected, but the process of emotional growth moves you into a broader community. You might discover others who are struggling to let go of the same loss you're struggling to free yourself from. You might find that your project works best when you collaborate or volunteer. And many organizations teach mindfulness. Restoring perspective is seldom if ever a solitary activity.

Taking the Long View

People who take the long view have a habit of seeing present circumstances in the context of their goals and objectives. For them, setbacks aren't failures. They are also able to revise certain objectives based on a realistic assessment of their performance without guilt.

Of course, taking the long view requires that you have identified goals and have an action plan for achieving them. In practice, your goals might not be entirely clear and your action plan might be only partially developed. What happens in the recovery process is that your goals become better defined and your plans take shape. As you do this work, you find that it becomes easier to use your ideas about where you are headed in the context for what is happening now.

Taking the long view consists of revising your goal. After you reflect on it, your new goal might be to enhance your social life, and losing fifty pounds would then be an objective toward that end. The long view in this case leads to a deeper understanding of why losing fifty pounds is important to you.

In the same way, a chronically anxious person might have a goal of overcoming agoraphobic tendencies by going to the library twice a week for the next four months thereby increasing his or her confidence in public settings. But after a good start, old habits can return and a few planned visits are missed. Taking the long view, this person revisits his or her goal. Simply going to the library had become boring. The goal needs to be embellished so that it included some social interaction.

Self-Care

Resistance is one strategy for blocking emotional growth; another more subtle strategy is indifference. Simply by complaining about being too tired or not motivated, you can sabotage any emotional growth plan. And you can do so while still giving lip service to your plan.

Self-care habits are many and varied. Among the habits most commonly mentioned are the following.

- Healthy sleep patterns
- Good diet

- Moderate exercise habits
- Regular work
- Diverse social network
- Ample time to relax
- Affirmative self-talk
- Laughter

In addition to these habits are others such as these.

- Cultivating a support system. It is hard to imagine a sustained emotional growth program without a fairly active support system.
- Taking the long view. It is important to let many frustrations and annoyances pass without response or to consider them in the light of long-term issues.
- Tolerate ambiguity. It helps to remember that many complex situations are seldom resolved by simple answers.

Perhaps the most valuable resource for sustaining emotional growth is trust. But trusting others when you have struggled to trust yourself and have been let down by others regularly is a difficult lesson. Though it sounds like a paradox, it is safe to say that progress in sustaining emotional growth depends on your willingness to be vulnerable to another person who will give you honest feedback. If you are lucky enough to have such a relationship, the rest of self-care will I suspect take care of itself.

Summary

The difference between restoring and sustaining emotional growth is the difference between learning skills and integrating them into your daily life. Restoring involves replacing one skill with another, a difficult undertaking. Sustaining is even more difficult because among other things, it requires the capacity to be flexible, to ask for help, to stay focused on your goal, and to take good care of yourself.

Advocates of the medical model don't typically distinguish between restoring and sustaining. Instead, they use medical terms such as *relapse* and *recurrence* to explain how symptoms return long after being treated. The idea that you can adjust to setbacks and learn from mistakes seems not to be considered; you either recover or fail to recover and start over.

Resistance is a normal human response to change. Its message is, don't try anything new—you might fail. This message comes in many disguises. Part of sustaining emotional growth is anticipating the subtle ways this message can present itself. Sustaining growth is also blocked by indifference to your own well-being. Combatting this obstacle calls for constant attention to self-care skills.

In the end, sustaining emotional growth requires trust. You need to learn skills including those outlined in this chapter, but skills—especially those that change your perspective—need to be nurtured. Perhaps a few people are entirely self-sufficient but most of us gain strength when others attend to our struggles. Before **we** can accept their support, we must trust that they have our best interests in mind. It is probably safe to say that trust is as difficult as any other aspect of emotional growth; lack of trust explains why so many people don't follow up with their plans.

Exercises
Sustaining Emotional Growth

Tendencies

Check the tendencies you have, and give examples of the tendencies you checked.

- Minimizing or discounting my accomplishments   _____
- Comparing myself unfavorably to my peers   _____
- Insisting on perfection in assessing myself   _____
- Being impatient   _____

Attitudes

Give examples of your sustaining attitudes by completing the following statements.

- I can take the long view because I know …
- When I feel vulnerable, I ask my friends for …
- I have a plan that isn't perfect, but …

Three Scenarios

The following exercises assume that you are engaged in an emotional growth task and have encountered obstacles while implementing your program. In each scenario, your response should refer to how you have used the skills discussed in this chapter.

Scenario 1: Becoming Discouraged

It is normal to become discouraged about your progress at some point in the course of an emotional growth program. If this has been your experience, you encountered resistance. Do you have a plan B?

Scenario 2: Becoming Distracted

If your personal resources are depleted and your daily life is filled with competing demands, it is difficult to concentrate on emotional growth. You are likely to be distracted.

Describe your distractions. Are your self-care habits secure enough to withstand the lure of those distractions?

Scenario 3: Losing Focus

Emotional growth is unlikely to occur in the absence of a support system. But if you have a history of depression, anxiety, or stress, you probably find trusting in others difficult. Do you have a support system? Have you used it? How can you improve your support system?

Chapter 6

Accepting Benefits

Introduction

This chapter is not about restoring perspective or sustaining emotional growth; it is about the consequences of sustaining emotional growth. It is one thing to learn skills whose purpose is to gain emotional distance, become more assertive, or enhance focus on your goals. It is quite another to realize that achieving your purposes even in some small way invites or challenges you to rethink your identity. I refer to these consequences as benefits. You might think that benefits are an unqualified asset but that is far from the truth. The benefits of emotional growth have their own peculiar logic. Consider two problems:

1. How to define benefits and
2. The consequences of accepting them.

Defining Benefits

Benefits are unique to each person. The best we can do is sketch broad categories of benefits. No single category will describe an individual's experience. With that in mind, I have outlined three types of benefits. Readers will have the opportunity to decide to what extent they fit into one of these categories and to what extent they are their own category.

I have distinguished three types of benefits though admittedly these types are somewhat arbitrary. The benefits encountered by any individual are unique. Nevertheless, for the purposes of this workbook, I will illustrate how you might recognize a benefit. The following diagram, Three Types of Benefits, outlines the emotional growth approach to benefits.

Three Types of Benefits

Types of Benefits Likely history	Qualitative Benefits	Quantitative Benefits	Spiritual Benefits
Life dominated by losses	Hope You feel liberated and imagine a revitalized future	Security You belong to a group whose members share your vision	Appreciation You are grateful for your gifts
Life dominated by dread	Confidence You feel competent to manage your –long-term issues and survive failures	Trust You bond with individuals who relate to your struggles.	Appreciation You embrace the reality of diverse experiences
Life dominated by difficulties with transitions	Peace of mind You have peace of mind and can express it	Focus You discover that staying in the present moment transcends temporal constraints	Appreciation You discover that meaning is found in daily routines

As noted, this diagram is illustrative of broad categories. Even so, it indicates a variety of ways to experience benefits. The background issues suggest that different emotional struggles might be associated with different types of benefits.

Qualitative Benefits

Qualitative benefits are characterized by feelings particularly hope, confidence, and peace of mind. For our purposes, each is defined below.

- Hope is the belief that your future won't replicate the patterns of past losses.
- Confidence is the belief that you can adopt habits that significantly enhance your capacity to implement your action plans.
- Peace of mind is a consequence of being mindful and perhaps other habits that enhance staying in the moment.

Almost forty years ago, I was recently divorced, in graduate school, and the custodial parent of my son; I was driving a cab on the weekends. My support system was largely gone as was my self-confidence. It was clearly time for me to start over.

I somehow completed a master's degree in social work and eventually found satisfactory employment with a foster-care agency, made some new friends, and learned how to be a single parent (at least I enjoyed time with my son). In time, I met my current wife and recovered my confidence.

In short, long before I knew anything about emotional growth, I was able to put the past behind me and adopt habits that built my confidence, and I did not let depression and anxiety keep me from growing. Though I never had a moment when hope or confidence became a reality for me, I now accept that both perspective-building skills enhanced my outlook on life.

The significance of qualitative benefits is that you recognize them not as an epiphany but as something transformative. Growth happens because you have done work to restore and sustain your perspective on the past, future, and present.

Quantitative Benefits

For some people, benefits are shared feelings. They occur because they are members of groups or communities that share their goals—ending world poverty, finding a cure for a particular disease, building a business, or improving the environment in some way are just a few examples. People who experience benefits in quantitative terms identify with a group and often express this identification with statements about what they believe or do.

Quantitative benefits differ from qualitative ones in that the former give meaning to everything else you do. Qualitative benefits enrich your personal experience, but they don't organize your life around a central theme from which meaning radiates. On the other hand, quantitative benefits do exactly that. You might feel hopeful, confident, or at peace with them, but you might also feel frustrated, isolated, or angry. They are benefits because they create meaning, not good feelings.

Unlike qualitative benefits, quantitative benefits can be described in literal terms. If my passion is to rid the park of litter or reduce the prevalence of poverty in Third World countries, I can quantify my purpose. I can measure the amount of litter picked up from year to year. I can refer to poverty statistics and note that the percent of youth in poverty has decreased in a certain country. These descriptions are relevant to my sense of accomplishment, and I can clearly share them with others. I cannot do so with qualitative benefits.

Spiritual Benefits

Some people experience emotional growth not as good feelings or as a source of meaning but rather as a sense that life itself is to be appreciated. These people might say that they appreciate the air they breathe, the sounds they hear, or the aromas they smell. They might say that they appreciate being pain free or that if they have pain that they have the capacity to feel anything. They might say that they appreciate the smile of a passing stranger, the companionship of a faithful pet, or the love of family and friends. If they encounter setbacks, they might say they appreciate the ability to explore the depth of their feelings. If they are cheated or betrayed, they appreciate the lessons learned and perhaps their capacity to learn lessons in the first place.

Appreciating is not the same as enjoying, and it is far removed from the belief that everything will turn out for the best. Just because you appreciate something does not mean it makes you happy. I appreciate my career failures, my first marriage and my aging body, not because they are wonderful things but because I learned, and continue to learn, that resolving issues is more important than feeling good. Besides, they remind me that we wouldn't enjoy springtime nearly so much without harsh winters.

The problem with appreciating is that it is normal to express appreciation, to feel grateful. You want to thank whoever is responsible for providing the many gifts you have been given. But how do you express your thanks? People who experience the benefits of emotional growth as gifts must work out the answer this question on their own terms.

As noted, the benefits of emotional growth are entirely personal and defy precise definitions. There is, however, an even more pressing problem with benefits: What happens if you accept them?

The Problem with Accepting Benefits

When you encounter a glimmer of hope, confidence or peace of mind why would anyone hesitate to embrace, or at least accept, that new feeling? If you have done the work of restoring and sustaining described in previous chapters it doesn't seem rational to refuse the benefits of that work. What is it about benefits that make some people turn away from them after doing so much to achieve them?

Consider the following. A depressed person manages to reframe his loss. He achieves emotional distance from his loss, say, the humiliation of a difficult divorce in which he lost primary custody of his child. The emotional distance, however, is rewarding. He puts the past firmly in the past and focuses on lessons learned. But in time, something new occurs, and he feels hope for the future. Not having had hope in a very long time, he hesitates and asks himself: Is this a trick or will this last if I acknowledge it? To be on the safe side, he, like many others, opts to discount the new feelings. The problem with accepting benefits is that you must choose between growth that is promising but risky and stability that is safe but boring.

Benefits are transformative. Many people who confront the choice hesitate, not out of fear of change but out of recognition that the time is not right for them to commit to a significant change. They might be preoccupied with pressing responsibilities or realize the need for a more active support system. Others might simply choose the security of the *status quo* and be wary of the uncertainty of change.

Accepting benefits is an act of faith. They aren't rewards for a job well done; nor are they consequences for adopting any particular skill. The only coherent way to conceptualize benefits is to understand them as "unscripted." People who express their benefits say that "they came out of the blue" or else as mysterious events for which they have no explanation.

In short, it is impossible to predict when benefits might occur or what shape they will take. If there is anything beyond the grasp of human reasoning it is the reality of benefits.

Summary

The benefits of emotional growth are profound; they draw you into a world in which values take precedence over coping with feelings and managing personal issues. Consider these benefits.

- Qualitative benefits introduce you to hope, confidence, and peace of mind, values that are consequences of restoring perspective and persevering when you are faced with obstacles.
- Quantitative benefits introduce you to security, trust, and focus. Security and trust are achieved in relation to shared goals with either groups or individuals with whom you

bond. Focus is quantitative only when you achieve clarity of purpose not found when temporal time is your only frame of reference.

- Spiritual benefits introduce you to appreciating daily life not in terms of your struggles with losses, failures, and disillusionment but in terms of values that give life meaning and accepting the totality of life experience as gifts and difficult experiences as lessons to be learned.

It is easy to understand why so many people struggle with benefits and, by extension, emotional growth. They do not submit to easy generalizations and they offer so much but at the same time demand so much of us.

Exercises

Discussion Topics

1. Why bother with the obscure and hard-to-define concept of benefits? Isn't it enough to restore and sustain emotional growth? Mainstream mental health discusses recovery but not the consequences of recovering. Why should emotional growth enter difficult territory?
2. Accepting benefits is difficult because of these factors.

- You should be careful what you wish for.
- You will always be disappointed when you encounter a benefit.
- You can't ever know enough about the future to know how benefits will turn out.

- You can't know what you give up when accepting benefits.

3. How can two people who encounter benefits of emotional growth have such different experiences? Is there something common to all benefits?

Chapter 7

Conclusion

Introduction

Thinking developmentally is an alternative to but not a substitute for the traditional and widely accepted medical model. It is an approach that recognizes troubling feelings as normal and struggles with loss, self-doubt and life transitions as unavoidable. It is characterized by the need to attend to your troubling feelings so you can discern the messages they convey and hence understand that your struggles are with issues, not feelings. It is further characterized by understanding that depressive and anxious feelings as well as chronic stress are essentially a loss of perspective and that ordinary, i.e. untrained, people can restore perspective with guidance and support. Finally, the point of emotional growth is to encounter benefits which, although they are difficult to understand and accept, offer the opportunity to find meaning in your everyday life.

I am persuaded that we need such an alternative for a variety of reasons including the following:

1. Emotional growth is accessible to a wider population than traditional mental health.
2. Emotional growth encourages personal initiative rather than medical treatment.
3. Emotional growth offers guidance and support

Emotional Growth Is Practical

It is skill based, and the skills involved are not technical. You can learn for example to reframe a loss that might have dominated your life and eroded your capacity to enjoy anything. Skeptics might ask that if emotional skills are practical, why are they so difficult to learn. Being practical should not be confused with being easy. It is consistent with asking for and accepting support, guidance, and for many, mental health counseling. Emotional growth is practical in the way that getting a college education before entering the workforce is practical.

Emotional Growth Is Purposeful

Emotional growth is not just about learning skills; it is also about selecting purposes. The purposes discussed in this workbook are broad goals: gaining emotional distance from your losses, being more assertive when confronting your challenges, and staying focused in the midst of life transitions. (See the emotional growth diagram on page 2). Your purposes might be variations on these themes, but whatever they are they are consequences of your personal initiative. That is, they are the answer to the question "Why are you making these changes?"

Emotional Growth Is Optimistic

Emotional growth does not promise happy endings, but it affirms your ability to learn, to interpret, to achieve and to join. Moreover, it promotes the idea that benefits are within the grasp of people who suffer with unwanted feelings. This is not, as discussed in the previous chapter, an unconditional guarantee. But if you believe that the work you do to restore your perspective and sustain your growth enhances your quality of life then you can expect to encounter gifts that, although quite real, defy rational description.

The Significance of Emotional Growth

I started by claiming that emotional growth has a claim on common sense because it is accessible to ordinary people. It is now possible to strengthen that claim. Emotional growth is common sense because it is practical, purposeful, and optimistic as long as you understand that each of these features involves its own kind of work. Perhaps the key to emotional growth is its emphasis on personal responsibility.

Assuming personal responsibility for your troubling feelings is central to any credible approach to mental health. Though well intentioned, the medical model produces profound and unnecessary obstacles in the lives of ordinary people seeking relief. Consider the following.

- It discourages independent initiative by insisting that mood disorders are rooted in physical defects. Yet many people who take initiative ask for help from friends who have no medical training and usually by trial and error work through all sorts of issues.
- It minimizes the role of guidance provided by peers and mentors. Guidance such as that presented in this workbook would be of no value simply because it is not medical.
- It discounts the capacity of ordinary people to grasp the messages conveyed by their troubling feelings and hence to distinguish between their feelings and their issues.

The value of emotional growth, then, is that it reintroduces personal responsibility into our understanding of mental health. No stigma is attached to saying that you participated in the development of your troubling feelings. That would be like attaching a stigma to being human. Yet by repeatedly making this assertion, the pharmaceutical industry has succeeded in empowering advocates of the medical model at the expense of ordinary people seeking relief from their persistent struggles.

I hope the day will come when emotional growth is as widely reflected of our culture as the medical model is today. I hope that the two models can exist together, the one focused on preventing the growth of emotional issues and the other dealing with those whose dysfunctional habits are so firmly entrenched that more-invasive interventions are the option of last resort. The reason for my optimism is as follows.

Emotional growth acknowledges your humanity, encourages you to be self-aware, challenges you to be purposeful, and invites you to be grateful. It is realistic about your limitations yet positive about your abilities. It affirms your capacity to understand your feelings and discern the issues they represent. It shows how being responsible for your feelings provides an incentive to address your issues. It describes skills that enable you to restore perspective on the past, the future, and the present so you can establish emotional distance from your losses, formulate realistic action plans, and maintain focus when your life seems chaotic. Finally, it helps you identify and appreciate the benefits of your initiatives.

Appendix A

How to Think Developmentally

Thinking developmentally consists of acquiring and using specific skills many of which have been discussed in this workbook. Readers can identify their skills with thinking developmentally by reviewing these lists and checking those they need to improve.

Skills

How to Understand Perspective

- **Expressive skill:** This skill enables you to express your troubling feelings in figurative language.
- **Exploring skill:** This skill enables you to contextualize your current feelings and look for coping patterns you have used.
- **Reflecting skill:** This skill consists of discerning your perspective based on your particular figurative language and the coping skills you have used.

How to Restore Perspective

- **Reframing:** This skill enables you to let go of your losses by changing the meaning of those experiences.
- **Adopting:** This skill enables you to build confidence by reinterpreting challenges into their component parts.
- **Being Mindful:** This skill enables you to focus on your goals by attending to the elements of your experience without judging or analyzing them.
- **Being Playful:** This skill enables bonding.

How to Integrate Emotional Growth

- **Being Affirmative:** When it becomes a habit, this skill enables you to directly confront resistance. It is a particularly difficult skill to adopt.
- **Anticipating Resistance:** When planning a program to restore perspective, it is always a good idea to have a backup plan ready.
- **Documenting Progress:** Since self-doubt tends to accompany resistance, it's a good habit to note in writing or on a calendar events that demonstrate specific accomplishments.
- **Taking the Long View:** The ability to distinguish feelings from issues and coping from management is evidence of this skill self-awareness skill.

How to Embrace the Benefits of Emotional Growth

- **Celebrate your gifts:** You have opportunities to appreciate life and show your gratitude.
- **Celebrate your resources:** You have friends who want your trust and who trust you.
- **Celebrate your progress:** You have grown. Allow yourself to enjoy the fact.

Purposes

Thinking developmentally is purposeful. Readers can formulate their own purposes by reviewing ones discussed in this workbook.

- If you are dealing with depressive feelings, your purpose might be to cultivate tools that prevent your losses from dominating your current life.
- If you are dealing with anxiety, your purpose might be to cultivate tools that allow you to be more assertive or to prevent fear of failure from dominating your current life.
- If you are dealing with chronic stress, your purpose might be to cultivate tools that enhance your ability to stay focused or prevent the distractions of daily life.

What is your purpose for wanting to grow emotionally?

Accepting Benefits

Thinking developmentally involves changing the way you define yourself. What have you done to adjust to the changes you have made? Have you

- Anticipated resistance to new habits?
- Asked a friend for feedback or guidance?
- Encountered a benefit?
- Shared your encounter?
- Joined a group that promotes the benefit you encountered?

Appendix B

Tell Your Developmental Story

The purpose of this workbook is to provide a framework that allows ordinary people to describe their emotional lives in nontechnical terms. A format for telling your story follows.

Section 1: What Happened?

Skill: Contextualizing Your Feelings

This section should consist entirely of factual statements as you recall them. What happened? When did it happen? Who knew about the events you are describing? What did they do? Did they help or harm you in their effort to help?

Don't worry about gaps in your memory. You will have the opportunity to discuss feeling about those facts in the following sections.

Section 2: How Do You Feel about What Happened?

Skill: Expressing Your Troubling Feelings

Use figurative language to put your feelings into words. Note that the metaphors you use convey messages about the past, future, and present. Also, note changes in how you feel about what happened. Have your feelings grown more intense? Are they more dominant, or have they subsided with the passage of time?

Section 3: What Coping Skills Have You Used?

Skill: Describe Your Short-Term Coping Skills

Did you suppress, procrastinate, mask, rationalize, or adopt some combination of these skills? Looking back, would you say the skills were helpful? Sometimes, short-term coping skills are helpful for a while, but then they become entrenched habits. What was your experience?

Section 4: What Are Your Goals?

Skill: Selecting a Long-Term Goal

The guidance model is a good place to start when thinking about goals. Did you have realistic goals when your emotional struggles began? Or did you just want to stop feeling bad? What are your current goals? Explain how you selected those goals.

Section 5: What Is Your Action Plan?

Skill: Adopting a Project with Goals and Objectives

At some point, you might have decided that short-term coping was not a plan. You started thinking strategically about your issues and how to find long-term relief from them. Review your previous responses; what action plan do you think might help you achieve your goal? Have you shared this plan with a friend? (Don't worry if your plan is sketchy; you can add details later.)

Section 6: What Obstacles Have You Encountered?

Skill: Dealing with Resistance

Plans invariably change when they come into contact with the real world and thus need to be revised and adjusted. Skills need to be improved. Support systems need to be strengthened. Most of all, you will find that new habits are difficult to implement and integrate into your daily life. What obstacles have you encountered?

Section 7: How Did You Overcome Those Obstacles?

Skill: Dealing with Acceptance

One of the most difficult parts of dealing with emotional issues is accepting new feelings. You might minimize them or discount them rather than accept new feelings, even feelings of hope, confidence, and peace of mind. Has this been your experience? Have you shared your struggle to accept new feelings with anyone?

Section 8: What Are the Benefits of Emotional Growth?

Skill: Appreciating Gifts

The goal of emotional growth is to appreciate experience as a gift. There are many ways to achieve this goal. You might for instance discover that hope, confidence, and peace of mind can be part of your daily life. You might discover that others share the project you have adopted and find meaning in the cooperative work you share. Or you might discover the spiritual quality of the relationships you form with others who are just as imperfect as you are.

Happiness is not a benefit of emotional growth; it is an occasional by-product of the work you do, not a goal as so many other accounts of emotional growth assume.

Appendix C

Three Problems for Further Discussion

As a framework, emotional growth should shed light on problems in the wider field of mental health. This section deals with three such problems. Discuss the pros and cons of each approach.

Problem 1: Helping People Who Don't Want to Be Helped

The central issue for people who aren't grounded is a lack of self-awareness. People who aren't grounded are totally unaware of how they interact with others. They might be bullies, manipulators, or chronic complainers, or they may simply be in need of constant recognition and affirmation. Other examples of not being grounded are idealists who see the world through rose-colored glasses, burnout survivors who haven't taken care of themselves while helping others, or cynics who lack the courage to trust anyone.

In a traditional mental health context, these conditions might be diagnosed as borderline personality disorders. In the context of emotional growth, people with these disorders aren't grounded. They lack the ability to talk about and explore their feelings;

they certainly don't own their feelings, so consequently, they are oblivious to the effect their behavior has on others much less their own emotionally neediness.

Question

Traditional mental health offers diagnoses so that the most effective treatment can be planned. In practice, this amounts to labeling problem behavior as a disorder and figuring what to do about the cause of that behavior.

Emotional growth offers an alternative approach. It proposes that you encourage troubled individuals to select a personal goal they can relate to and follow up with an action plan for achieving that goal. This strategy avoids any labeling or suggestion of biological defects that might interfere with a productive intervention. Which approach would you recommend?

Problem 2: The Medicalization of Troubling Feelings

People who complain of feeling depressed, anxious, or chronically stressed are often advised to make an appointment with a physician or other qualified medical professional to get a diagnosis. The assumption is that troubling feelings are caused by biochemical defects; ordinary untrained people are not qualified to discern the connections between physical states in the body and symptoms reported by a distressed person.

Emotional growth suggests that people who are depressed, anxious, or stressed can identify their troubling feelings and perhaps with guidance recognize the messages conveyed by those feelings. They might be able to explain their feelings in terms of a relevant context or by their pattern of coping.

Question

Mainstream mental health assumes that depression, anxiety, and chronic stress are consequences of biological defects and that those defects can (or must) be treated as any other medical problem is. Emotional growth assumes that depression, anxiety, and chronic stress are consequences of a lack of perspective on your losses, challenges, or turbulent circumstances and that many people who struggle can identify their issues and take steps to restore their perspective. Which approach would you recommend?

Problem 3: The Trivializing of Recovery

Advocates of the medical model define recovery as improved symptom management. This definition works for them because symptom management can be quantified. Behavioral improvements can be measured in terms of how frequently a symptom occurs, how long it lasts, and how severe it is on a scale of 1 to 10. If you can manage your troubling symptoms better than you did before treatment started, you have recovered or at least made progress toward recovery.

Emotional growth dispenses with the need to quantify mental health. If you cultivate habits that restore perspective and sustain those habits, you can expect that your initiatives will have consequences. The consequences, however, are complicated human experiences not subject to quantification. For one thing, we tend to resist growth because it presents new experiences. For another, we don't encounter real-life problems according to a schedule. In fact, it isn't even clear how to describe encounters with hope, confidence, or peace of mind.

Question

We know from life experiences that people who have struggled with enormous emotional difficulties have overcome great obstacles and even transformed their identities. Is it possible to explain these realites if recovery is defined as improved symptom management, or do we need an alternative account such as the one offered by emotional growth?

Appendix D

A Sample Reading List of Mental Health Literature

The Medical Model

Randy J. Patterson. 2002. *Your Depression Map: Find the Source of Your Depression and Chart Your Own Course*. Oakland, CA: New Harbinger Publications.

Peter Kramer, 2005. *Against Depression*. New York: Penguin Group.

Cognitive Behavior Therapy

David Burns. 1980. *Feeling Good: The New Mood Therapy*. New York: HarperCollins.

Zindal V. Segal, J. Mark, G. Williams, and John S. Teasdale. 2002. *Mindfulness-Based Cognitive Therapy for Depression: A new Approach for Preventing Relapse*. New York: Guilford Press.

James P. McCullough, Jr. 2000. *Treatment of Chronic Depression: Cognitive Behavioral Analysis System of Psychotherapy*. The Guilford Press. New York NY

New Age Approaches

Deepak Chopra. 1991. *Unconditional Life: Mastering the Forces that Shape Personal Reality*. New York: Harper Collins.

Thomas Moore. 1992. *Care of the Soul: A Guide to Cultivating Depth and Sacredness in Everyday Life*. New York: Harper Collins.

Personal Accounts

Jeffrey Wilson. 2004. *Irrational Medicine*. Grove City, OH: Garcia Press.

Holistic Approaches

Gabriel Cousens, with Mark Mayell. 2001. *Depression-Free for Life: A Physician's All Natural 5-Step Plan*. New York: Harper Collins.

Emotional Pain Model

Ty Colbert. 1966. *Broken Brains or Wounded Hearts: What Causes Mental Illness*. Santa Ana, CA: Kevco Publishing.

Workbooks

G. Allen Marshall and Deborah S. Romaine. 2008. *Changing Old Habits for Good: Break Free from Habits That Hold You Back*. New York: Alpha Books.

Steven C. Hayes and Spencer Smith. 2005. *Get Out of Your Mind and into Your Life: The New Acceptance and Commitment Therapy*. Oakland, CA: New Harbinger Press.

About the Author

While mental health has become increasingly technical, relying on various medical models or esoteric accounts about the nature of the universe, Mr. Watkins hopes this practical account of emotional growth will encourage readers to rely on the resources they have at hand.

My career as a social worker in foster care, community mental health and school-based services convinced me that most text book accounts of emotional struggles present obstacles for many clients and sometimes discourage them from making purposeful changes. I believe clients are more responsive when they take ownership of their issues and have realistic plans for change.

With these considerations in mind, Mr. Watkins has put together an easy to follow outline whose purpose is to guide "ordinary" people in their struggles to with depressive, anxious and stressful feelings. Although this workbook is not for everyone, my hope is that many readers will find it useful.

Printed in the United States
By Bookmasters